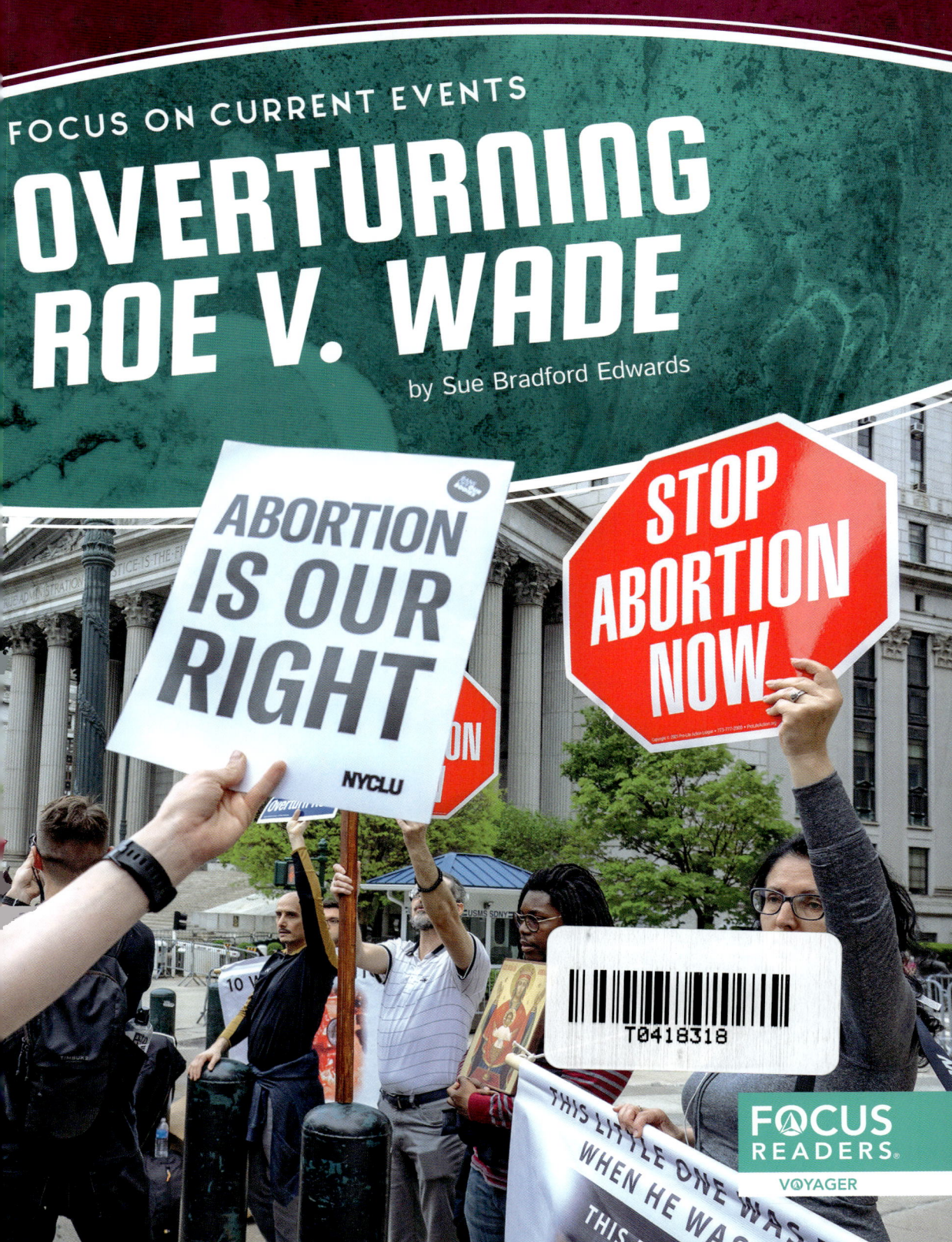

www.focusreaders.com

Copyright © 2024 by Focus Readers®, Lake Elmo, MN 55042. All rights reserved. No part of this book may be reproduced or utilized in any form or by any means without written permission from the publisher.

Focus Readers is distributed by North Star Editions:
sales@northstareditions.com | 888-417-0195

Produced for Focus Readers by Red Line Editorial.

Content Consultant: Alicia Gutierrez-Romine, PhD, Associate Professor of History, La Sierra University

Photographs ©: Ron Adar/SOPA Images/Sipa USA/AP Images, cover, 1; Zach Brien/NurPhoto/AP Images, 4–5; Patsy Lynch/MediaPunch/IPX/AP Images, 7; Jim Wells/AP Images, 8–9; Bill Janscha/AP Images, 10; AP Images, 13; iStockphoto, 14–15, 21; Rich Sugg/The Kansas City Star/AP Images, 17; Red Line Editorial, 19, 45; Rogelio V. Solis/AP Images, 22–23; Evelyn Hockstein/Reuters/Alamy, 25; Erin Schaff/Pool/The New York Times/AP Images, 27; Shutterstock Images, 28–29, 31, 32, 36, 41; Allen G. Breed/AP Images, 34–35; Charlie Riedel/AP Images, 39; Darron Cummings/AP Images, 42–43

Library of Congress Cataloging-in-Publication Data
Library of Congress Cataloging-in-Publication Data is available on the Library of Congress website.

ISBN
978-1-63739-643-8 (hardcover)
978-1-63739-700-8 (paperback)
978-1-63739-807-4 (ebook pdf)
978-1-63739-757-2 (hosted ebook)

Printed in the United States of America
Mankato, MN
082023

ABOUT THE AUTHOR
Sue Bradford Edwards is a Missouri nonfiction author. She writes about current events, social sciences, natural sciences, and history. She is the author of more than 30 titles for young readers. Her books include *What Are Learning Disorders?*, *Become a Construction Equipment Operator*, *Being Black in America*, and *Robotics in Health Care*.

TABLE OF CONTENTS

CHAPTER 1
Protest at the Supreme Court 5

CHAPTER 2
Roe v. Wade 9

CHAPTER 3
After *Roe* 15

CASE STUDY
Planned Parenthood v. Casey 20

CHAPTER 4
Dobbs v. Jackson Women's Health Organization 23

CHAPTER 5
Arguments Against Abortion Rights 29

CHAPTER 6
Arguments for Abortion Rights 35

CASE STUDY
Abortion Access Across Genders 40

CHAPTER 7
After *Dobbs* 43

Focus on Overturning *Roe v. Wade* • 46
Glossary • 47
To Learn More • 48
Index • 48

CHAPTER 1

PROTEST AT THE SUPREME COURT

On June 24, 2022, protesters gathered outside the US Supreme Court. As the day went on, more and more people arrived. The protesters were reacting to a decision the court had made that day. It had ruled 6–3 in *Dobbs v. Jackson Women's Health Organization*. This decision overturned an earlier case called *Roe v. Wade*. It ruled that the US Constitution did not protect the right to an **abortion**.

Supporters of abortion rights protest outside the Supreme Court on June 24, 2022.

The protesters weren't all in agreement. One group supported abortion rights. Some people carried signs. One sign read, "Bans off our bodies." Another read, "Abortion is health care." One read, "My body, my choice." This group believed it was standing up for women's health.

Anti-abortion protesters also gathered. They carried signs, too. One of these signs read, "Human rights begin in the womb." One read, "One-third of my generation has been killed by abortion." Another read, "Love them both." These protesters believed they were protecting lives.

For both sides, the fall of *Roe* was massively important. The Supreme Court had decided *Roe* in 1973. Anti-abortion activists had been working to overturn it for nearly 50 years. They viewed its fall as a major victory. They believed they had succeeded in protecting human life.

▲ Opponents of abortion rights celebrate outside the Supreme Court on June 24, 2022.

For people who supported abortion rights, the fall of *Roe* was devastating. Having a baby changes the parent's life. The ability to access legal abortions gives pregnant people more control. And for nearly 50 years, abortion had been largely legal. The *Dobbs* decision made abortion a crime again in many states. It took choice away from pregnant people. They had less control over their bodies.

CHAPTER 2

ROE V. WADE

Abortions were generally legal during the early years of the United States. They were even common early on in a pregnancy. However, lawmakers began banning abortion in the mid-1800s. By the early 1900s, the practice was illegal across the country.

Laws changed slightly in the 1960s. Some states allowed abortion in medical emergencies. But it remained a crime in most states.

Florynce "Flo" Kennedy's work as a lawyer helped New York State legalize abortion in 1970.

▲ Jane Roe's real name was Norma McCorvey.

In 1970, a woman filed a lawsuit. She was called Jane Roe to hide her real name. Roe filed the suit against Henry Wade. He was the district attorney of Dallas County, Texas, where Roe lived. Under Texas law, people needed their doctors' approval to have abortions. The doctor had to agree it would save the patient's life. Roe wanted an abortion. She said she should not need a doctor's approval. The US Supreme Court heard the lawsuit in 1973.

Lawyers for Texas made two main points. First, they pointed to the Fourteenth **Amendment** to the Constitution. This amendment says states cannot take away a person's life without a fair legal process. Texas's lawyers argued a **fetus** is a person. So, they said the Fourteenth Amendment protects fetuses.

Second, the lawyers pointed to the term *compelling state interest*. A *state interest* is any public issue that governments manage. In this case, *compelling* means "necessary." The lawyers argued that states have a compelling interest in protecting life. Then they argued that life begins at **conception**. So, they said the state interest in protecting life begins at conception.

Lawyers speaking for Roe made two main points of their own. First, they said the Fourteenth Amendment protects citizens' freedom. They claimed Texas's abortion law took away a woman's freedom. Second, they argued the law took away a woman's privacy. They said the Constitution promised privacy to citizens.

The Supreme Court ruled in favor of Roe. It made abortion legal. It held that the Constitution protects the right to an abortion. It said Texas's laws went against the Constitution. The court also said the Constitution does not protect fetuses. But it said the Constitution does not promise the right to an abortion in all cases. It said states should guard human health and possible life. The court decided these state interests mattered.

▲ Justice Harry Blackmun (top right) wrote the Supreme Court's opinion for *Roe v. Wade*.

The court tried to balance states' interests and people's right to privacy. It divided pregnancy into three 12-week stages. Each stage is called a trimester. During the first trimester, states cannot ban abortion. During the second, states may limit abortion for health reasons. During the third, states can ban abortion. The court also said a woman can have an abortion at any time during the pregnancy to protect her life or health.

CHAPTER 3

AFTER *ROE*

The impact of *Roe v. Wade* was significant. Abortion was no longer a crime. Before *Roe*, police targeted health-care workers who performed abortions. Police also used health-care workers to report abortions. The **criminal justice system** and health-care system were connected. *Roe* helped separate the two systems. Patients' civil rights improved as a result. Seeking health care involved less risk of going to jail.

Trust between doctors and patients is an important part of effective health care.

Roe also greatly increased legal abortions. This shift led to much safer and less-expensive abortions. These changes had the biggest impact for low-income women, women of color, and unmarried women. These groups became better able to access abortions. As a result, *Roe* increased gender and racial equality in the United States. Women gained more control in their own lives. They were better able to hold jobs. Having their own money gave women more independence.

However, not everyone approved of *Roe*. The ruling helped an anti-abortion movement grow. This movement was **conservative**. It believed abortion rights threatened traditional gender roles. Gender roles are the social behaviors that a culture expects of certain genders.

Some anti-abortion activists protested at women's health clinics. Others turned to violence.

▲ In 2009, an anti-abortion activist murdered George Tiller, a doctor who provided abortions in Kansas.

From 1977 to 2020, protesters set nearly 200 clinics on fire. They bombed 42 others. They also murdered 11 clinic workers.

The anti-abortion movement worked on new laws as well. For example, Congress passed the Hyde Amendment in 1976. This law stopped Medicaid from paying for nearly all abortions. Medicaid is health insurance offered to low-income people. As a result of the law, low-income people had less access to abortion.

Anti-abortion activists also built a legal movement. This movement worked to make the legal system more conservative. It helped conservative lawyers, judges, and law professors. It also brought challenges to *Roe*. States passed laws that limited abortion. The laws led to lawsuits. Conservative lawyers defended the laws. Some cases made it to the Supreme Court.

At the same time, an abortion rights movement grew. It formed in part from the civil rights and women's rights movements. Lawyers challenged new abortion laws in court. Activists raised money for people wanting abortions. Others helped pregnant people get to clinics. They kept people safe from anti-abortion activists.

In addition, many activists of color worked to reframe abortion. They talked about it as part of a larger issue. They used the term *reproductive justice*. This included abortion. It focused on racism and sexism in health care. But it also focused on parenthood, sexual education, and more.

Even so, the Supreme Court weakened *Roe* over the decades. By the 2010s, most counties had zero abortion providers. Several states had only one clinic. The Midwest and South saw the largest declines in abortion providers.

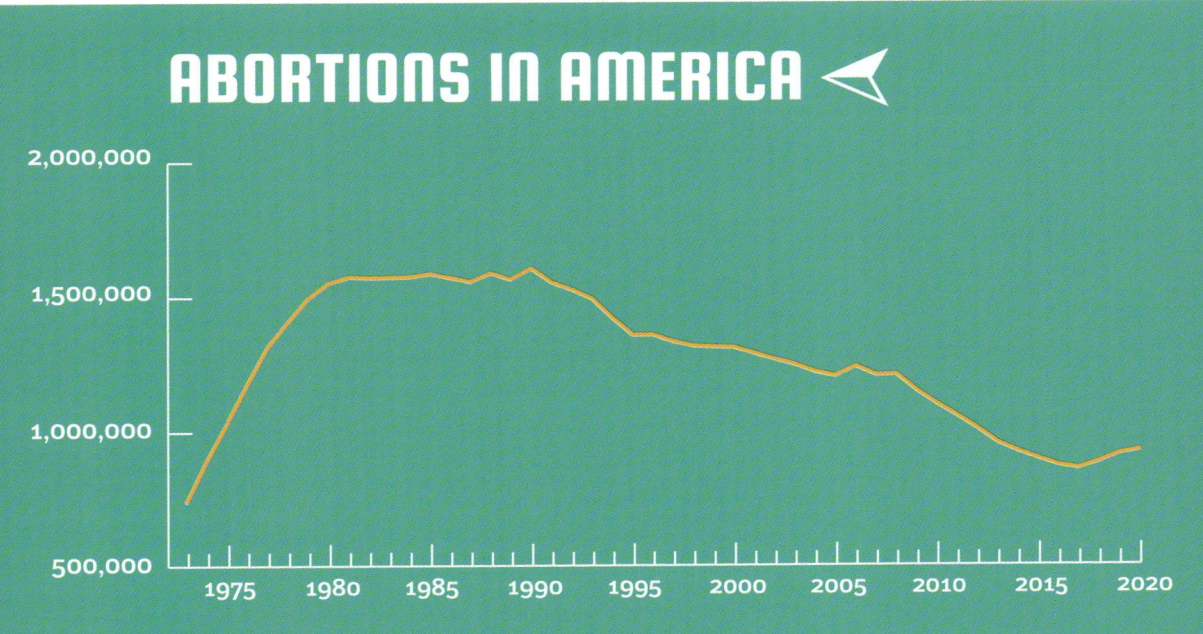

ABORTIONS IN AMERICA

CASE STUDY

PLANNED PARENTHOOD V. CASEY

In 1992, the Supreme Court ruled on *Planned Parenthood v. Casey*. A Pennsylvania law had passed in 1989. It required counseling before an abortion. It required a one-day waiting period. Also, people under 18 needed a parent's permission. Clinics challenged the law.

The Supreme Court upheld *Roe*. But it weakened parts of the ruling. For example, *Roe*'s trimester system became far less important. This made early abortions less protected. Instead, the court used the term *undue burden*. In the ruling, *undue* meant "extreme." *Burden* meant "a barrier." The court said no law could place an undue burden on a woman who wanted an abortion.

▲ Barriers to abortion access can be especially high for low-income women and women of color.

However, the court did not clearly define what was or wasn't an undue burden. As a result, states passed many laws limiting abortion. *Casey* also kept parts of Pennsylvania's law. For example, it kept the one-day waiting period. The court did not consider that an undue burden.

Abortion-rights supporters disagreed. Suppose a low-income woman lives far from a clinic. Traveling there costs money. And taking time off work means no income that day. With a waiting period, the woman might need two trips. The costs might become too high.

CHAPTER 4

DOBBS V. JACKSON WOMEN'S HEALTH ORGANIZATION

In March 2018, Mississippi passed a new law. It was called the Gestational Age Act. This law banned abortion after the fetus is 15 weeks old. The law stated that a fetus begins to take human form at 15 weeks. However, critics disagreed. They noted that there is no scientific evidence for this claim.

The law also said an abortion is a risk to the woman's health. Critics said this claim was also

A Mississippi lawmaker debates the Gestational Age Act in March 2018.

wrong. They pointed to a 2012 study. It showed that few women have physical problems after an abortion. The study also showed that abortion is 14 times safer than giving birth.

Hours after the law was passed, the Jackson Women's Health Organization filed a lawsuit. This clinic was Mississippi's only abortion provider. It wanted to keep the law from going into effect. That's because the law would likely force the clinic to close. The suit was called *Dobbs v. Jackson Women's Health Organization*. Thomas E. Dobbs was Mississippi's state health officer.

A court in Mississippi heard the case. The court ruled that the law was not legal. It said the law went against *Roe v. Wade*. The court also said laws that limit abortion need to be based on medicine. The state could block abortion only if the fetus was viable. This means the fetus must be able to

▲ The Jackson Women's Health Organization's clinic was called the Pink House. It closed in July 2022.

survive outside the **uterus**. A fetus often reaches this point at about 24 weeks.

The state of Mississippi appealed the ruling. It asked a higher court to reverse the ban. However, the higher court agreed with the earlier ruling. It said the law was not medically sound.

So, Mississippi appealed again. This brought the case to the US Supreme Court.

The Supreme Court did not look at the wording of the Mississippi law. It did not consider whether the law was based on medical facts. Instead, the Supreme Court reviewed older rulings. It looked at *Roe v. Wade*. It also reviewed *Planned Parenthood v. Casey*. These cases said the Constitution protected abortion rights. However, the court noted that the Constitution does not talk about abortion. In addition, the court said the right to abortion is not part of early US history. Many history experts disagreed. They noted

➤ THINK ABOUT IT

How large a role do you think medicine and science should play in Supreme Court decisions? Why?

▲ Justice Samuel Alito (lower left) wrote the Supreme Court's opinion for *Dobbs*.

that abortion was legal throughout much of the country's early years.

On June 24, 2022, the Supreme Court voted. It overruled the lower courts. Mississippi's Gestational Age Act would stand. *Roe v. Wade* was overturned. *Planned Parenthood v. Casey* was overturned as well. States now had more ability to ban abortions.

CHAPTER 5

ARGUMENTS AGAINST ABORTION RIGHTS

People make many arguments against abortion rights. One common argument is that abortion is murder. The argument often has two parts. Most people agree with the argument's first part. It says that all human life should be protected equally. For this reason, taking an innocent life is murder. Governments must help protect against murder.

Anti-abortion protesters march with signs in May 2022.

The argument's second part is more **controversial**. This part argues that full human life begins before birth. Some anti-abortion advocates say life begins at conception. Others say it begins when a fetus is viable. A full human life must be protected. Anti-abortion advocates argue that abortion takes away a full human life. Therefore, they believe it is murder. They say the government must prevent abortions.

Supporters of abortion rights disagree with this position in two ways. One disagreement is about when a human life begins. Some people believe life begins at birth. Others say it begins many weeks after conception. The other disagreement involves equality. Supporters of abortion rights argue that governments should protect the pregnant person's rights. They argue that an **embryo** or fetus should not matter more than the

⏶ The Catholic Church has long opposed abortion.

person who is pregnant. Rather, pregnant people should be able to choose.

    Some people reach their position through religion. For example, many Jews believe human life begins at birth. In contrast, many Christians believe life begins at conception. For these Christians, abortion goes against their religious beliefs. Many supporters of abortion rights point to the Constitution. It says religion should be

▲ The US Constitution lays out the country's basic laws and beliefs. It has been in effect since 1789.

separate from the government. So, they argue that religion should not be the basis for abortion laws.

Other arguments are about the pregnant person. For instance, some anti-abortion advocates say abortions are unsafe. However, this claim is not medically true. Abortions are some of the safest medical procedures. Anti-abortion advocates also say abortions harm pregnant people in other ways. They say people often regret having abortions.

Some anti-abortion arguments take a legal route. They argue that the Constitution does not mention abortion rights. Instead, they say the issue should be left to states. Or they might say abortion rights cannot exist without an amendment to the Constitution. One example could be the Equal Rights Amendment (ERA). This amendment would guarantee equal rights for all genders. For this reason, it would likely protect abortion rights. People opposed to abortion might also oppose the ERA. But they argue that having it would more clearly define abortion rights.

THINK ABOUT IT

Some laws allow actions that go against certain people's individual beliefs. How should lawmakers consider personal beliefs when making new laws?

NDC: 43393-001-06

Mifepristone Tablets

200 mg

Rx only
Contains 6 Cartons
Each Carton Contains 1 Tablet

GenBioPro

Dispense the Medication Guide provided separately to each patient.

NDC: 43393-001-06

Mifepristone Tablets

200 mg

Rx only
Contains 6 Cartons
Each Carton Contains 1 Tablet

GenBioPro

Dispense the Medication Guide provided separately to each patient.

CHAPTER 6

ARGUMENTS FOR ABORTION RIGHTS

People make a variety of arguments in support of abortion rights. One argument focuses on medicine. Abortions can be necessary to save the pregnant person. Some abortion bans still allow abortions when they are medically necessary. But these laws can make doctors hesitate. Such delays can lead to more health problems. For this reason, supporters argue for greater abortion rights.

More than half of abortions use medication. They usually use two pills, the first being mifepristone.

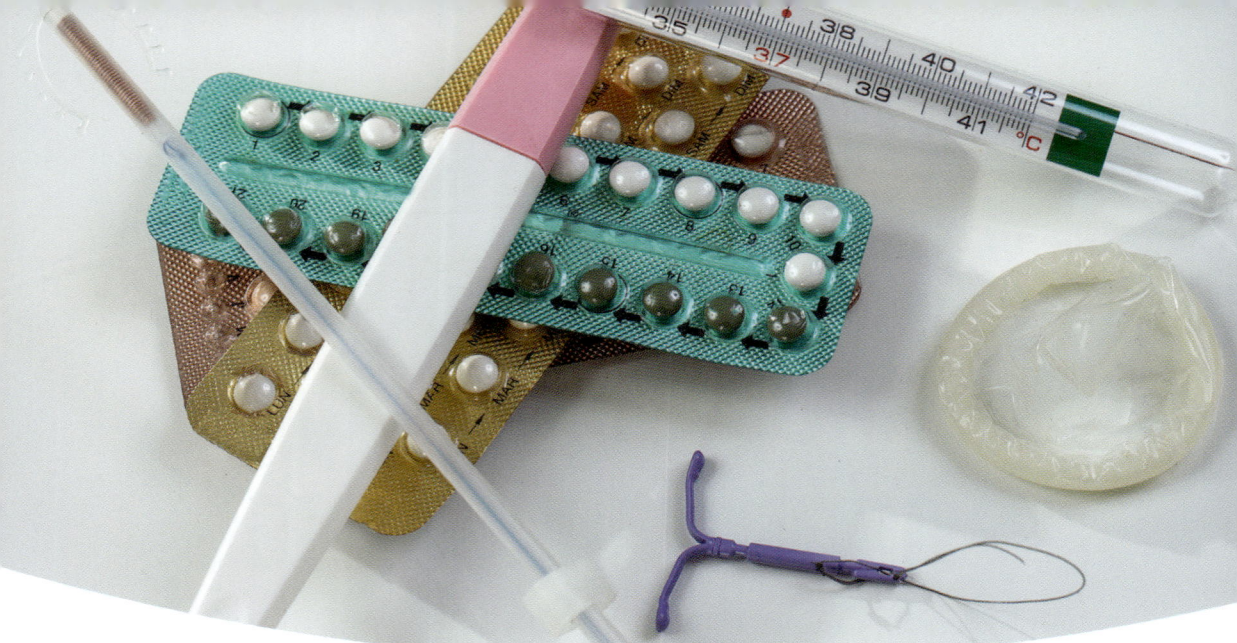

▲ Birth control helps sexually active people avoid pregnancy. But unintended pregnancy is still common.

Also, people have many reasons for not wanting to become pregnant. Some people do not want to be parents. Others do, but they want to plan. They might need a more stable income. They might want to wait for marriage. Young people tend to want to wait until they are adults. In addition, many people already have children. But more children are not in their family plans. For these reasons, supporters say access to legal abortion is essential. They argue that it gives people power over their bodies and lives.

Opponents of abortion argue this power shouldn't be needed. Also, they often believe that sex before marriage is wrong. So, they say women should just not have sex. Then they won't need an abortion. However, abortion-rights supporters argue that sexual assault can lead to pregnancy. Then, people are not in control.

People who support abortion rights also point to research. In one study, researchers talked to women who wanted abortions. Some women went on to have them. Others were denied abortions. Five years later, most women who'd had an abortion believed they had made the right decision. They had fewer mental health issues.

In contrast, women who were denied abortions had harder lives. They were more likely to face poverty. They were more likely to have stayed with abusive partners. They were more likely to have health problems. And their children suffered.

In response, abortion opponents might use one of their main arguments. They say that abortion is murder. It might be true that not having one can be hard. But they argue that difficulty does not make murder acceptable.

Abortion-rights supporters also make a **feminist** argument. They argue that abortion bans turn women into second-class citizens. That's because abortion mainly affects women. By forcing women to give birth, states are limiting

➤ THINK ABOUT IT

Do you think abortion is health care? Or is it something else? Explain your argument.

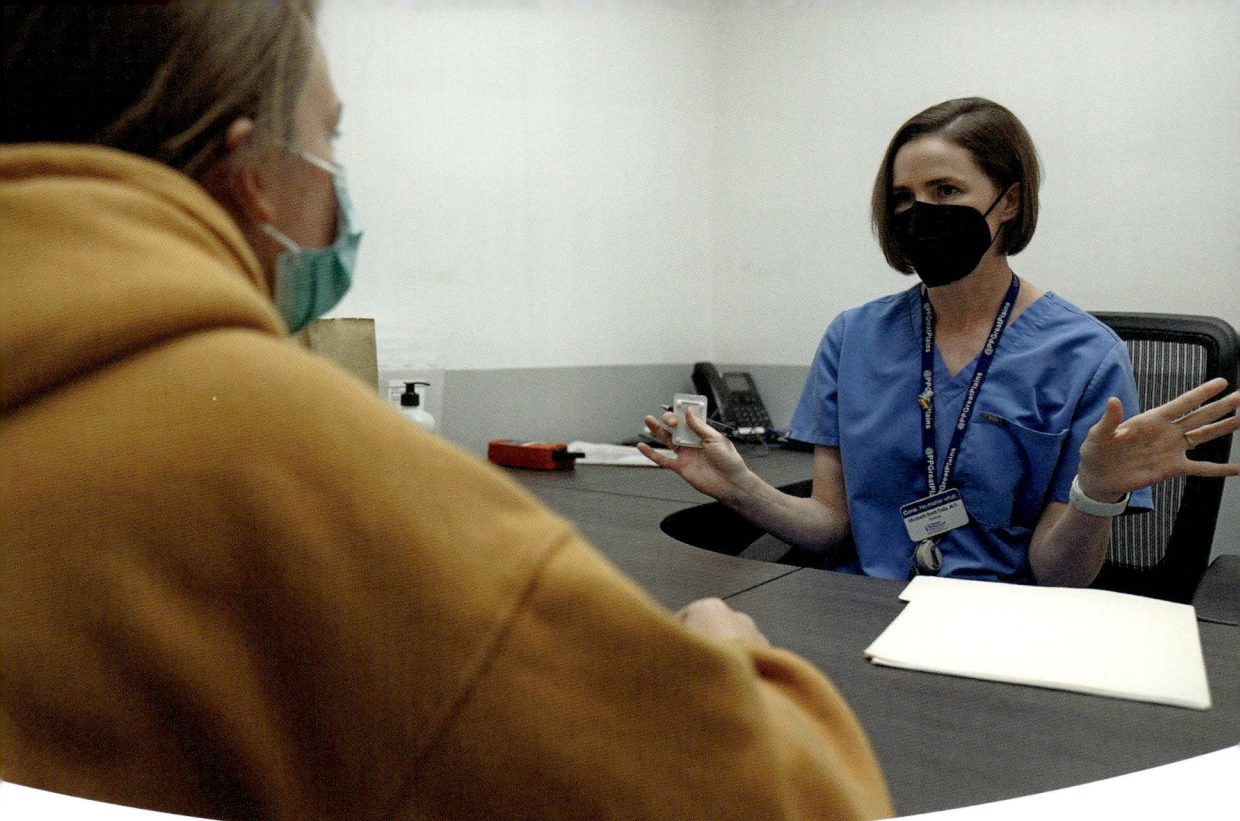

▲ In 2020, there were 807 clinics in the United States that provided abortions.

women's choices. As a result, anti-abortion laws increase gender inequality.

People who oppose abortion often point to traditional family values. They argue that men and women have gender roles. They say women should be wives and mothers. They say the choices that abortions offer to women can harm the family.

CASE STUDY

ABORTION ACCESS ACROSS GENDERS

Debates over abortion often focus on women and girls. In part, this focus is because abortion laws typically mention women only. They tend to follow a binary idea of gender. The gender binary is the idea that there are only two genders. It says people are either male or female.

However, people's identities often do not fit into this idea of gender. For example, many people identify as trans or nonbinary. Trans people have a different gender than they were assigned at birth. Nonbinary people have genders that are neither male nor female. They can be in between the two. Or they can be something completely different.

Many pregnant trans men and nonbinary people struggle to access abortions. These groups are more likely to be harassed, including while

▲ Trans and nonbinary identities represent just part of the variety of people's gender identities.

seeking health care. They are more likely to face violence, too.

In addition, abortion clinics are more likely to provide health care that trans people need. Other places often do not. When laws force these clinics to close, trans people can lose access to many kinds of health care.

CHAPTER 7

AFTER DOBBS

The overturning of *Roe v. Wade* had swift impacts. Several states had trigger laws. Trigger laws are laws that have already been passed. But they do not take effect unless other legal changes occur. For these laws, the trigger was overturning *Roe*. After that happened, trigger laws in 13 states banned most abortions. Laws in three states went into effect 30 days after the *Dobbs* ruling. Others took effect right away.

In 2022, Indiana's attorney general wanted to punish a doctor who provided an abortion to a 10-year-old rape survivor.

Some trigger laws were blocked. For instance, North Dakota's only abortion clinic challenged the state's trigger law. Even so, the clinic did not want to risk losing the case. So, it moved across the border to Minnesota. Abortion remained protected in that state.

Within months, trigger laws had affected millions of people. Abortion costs increased. People often had to travel much farther to get one. They often had to go to states where it was protected. As a result, those states were also affected. Demand increased quickly.

After *Dobbs*, several states put abortion rights on the ballot. In August 2022, people in Kansas voted on changing the state constitution. The amendment would have banned abortion statewide. But Kansas voters chose not to ban abortion. In November, five more states voted on the issue. In each state, voters chose in favor of more abortion rights rather than fewer.

In 2022, 62 percent of Americans believed abortion should be legal in all or most cases. Thirty-six percent thought the opposite. The debate over abortion was not over.

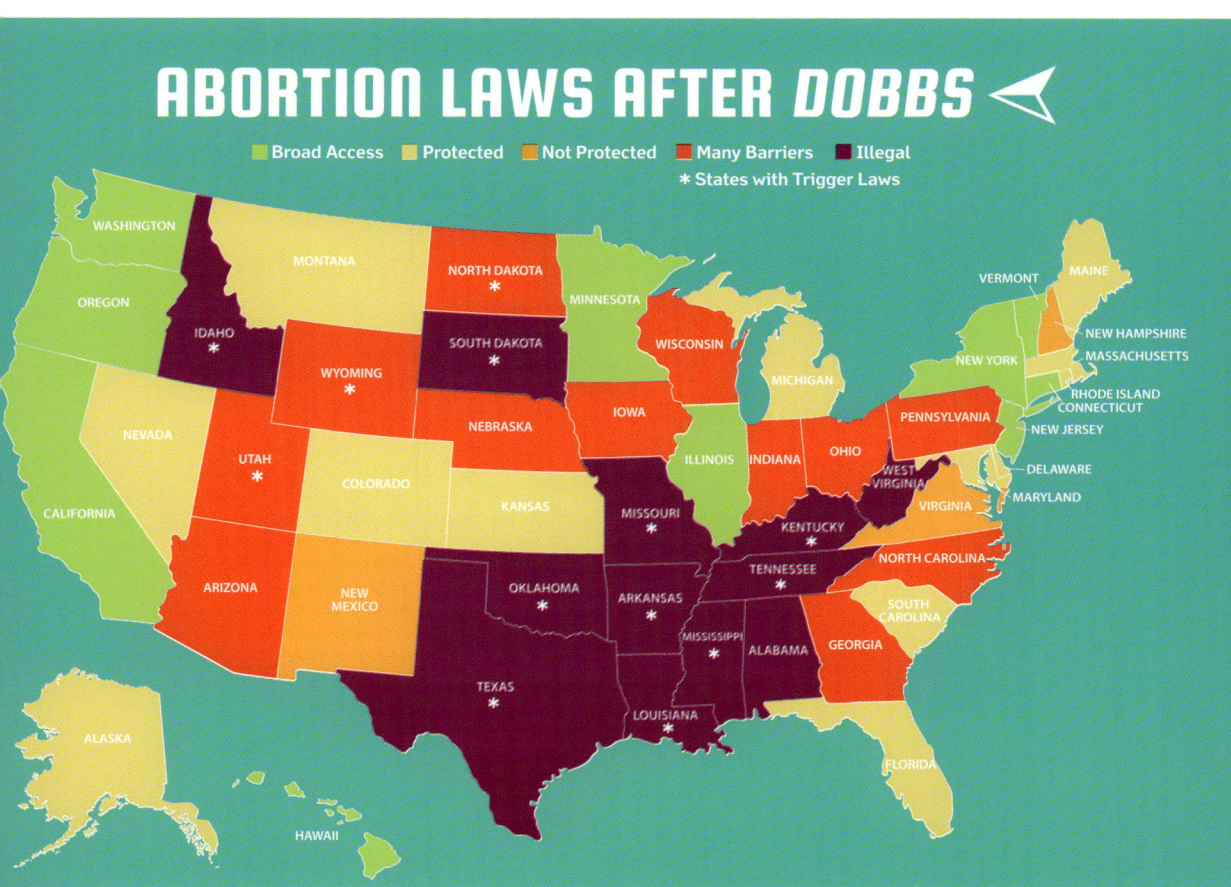

FOCUS ON OVERTURNING ROE V. WADE

Write your answers on a separate piece of paper.

1. Write a paragraph that explains the main ideas of Chapter 2.

2. What laws, if any, do you think should exist about abortion? Why?

3. Which case overturned *Roe v. Wade*?
    - **A.** *Dobbs v. Jackson Women's Health Organization*
    - **B.** *Planned Parenthood v. Casey*
    - **C.** the Hyde Amendment

4. Why did overturning *Roe v. Wade* have such quick impacts?
    - **A.** Abortion became illegal in every state after the ruling.
    - **B.** Residents in every state voted on abortion rights soon afterward.
    - **C.** Many states had trigger laws that took effect afterward.

Answer key on page 48.

GLOSSARY

abortion
A medical end to a pregnancy, either by medication or through a procedure.

amendment
A change or addition to a legal document.

conception
The process of becoming pregnant.

conservative
Supporting traditional views or values, often resisting changes.

controversial
Likely to be argued about.

criminal justice system
The system of rules, processes, and agencies that manage crime and enforce an area's laws.

embryo
A beginning stage of a developing animal.

feminist
Supporting equal rights for all genders.

fetus
A development stage of animals with backbones, when the animal has become its basic form. For humans, this stage happens after the embryo stage.

uterus
An organ that holds the fetus as it develops during pregnancy.

TO LEARN MORE

BOOKS

Ford, Jeanne Marie. *Understanding Reproductive Health*. Minneapolis: Abdo Publishing, 2021.

Mihaly, Christy. *Defining and Discussing Women's Rights*. North Mankato, MN: Rourke Educational Media, 2020.

Mooney, Carla. *Overturned: The Constitutional Right to Abortion*. San Diego: ReferencePoint Press, 2022.

NOTE TO EDUCATORS

Visit www.focusreaders.com to find lesson plans, activities, links, and other resources related to this title.

INDEX

Constitution, 5, 11–12, 26, 31, 33

Dobbs v. Jackson Women's Health Organization, 5–7, 24–27, 43–45

Equal Rights Amendment (ERA), 33

Fourteenth Amendment, 11–12

Gestational Age Act, 23–27

Hyde Amendment, 17

Kansas, 44–45

Minnesota, 44–45
Mississippi, 23–27, 45

North Dakota, 44–45

Pennsylvania, 20–21, 45

Planned Parenthood v. Casey, 20–21, 26–27

Roe, Jane, 10–12

Supreme Court, 5–6, 11–13, 18–19, 20–21, 26–27

Texas, 10–12, 45

Answer Key: 1. Answers will vary; 2. Answers will vary; 3. A; 4. C